Inspirational Writings

By

Christopher Marshall

Contents

Introduction

I first joined a Spiritual development circle in 2004 and from the first we were asked to do 'Homework'; that is at some time between the weekly circles we were to sit in the quiet and ask our guides for some inspirational words.

What follows is a collection of the words I have written down for such exercises, and these date from 2004 to 2014. They are not presented in any particular order, nor are they organised by theme. You may read them in any order or may work systematically from the beginning to the end, perhaps marking in the table of contents those that are your favourites.

Some of these are simply messages of encouragement, others of comfort, and still more are for instruction. In proof reading it seems that a theme is running through them all. Don't be discouraged. Each message should give you pause for thought, and if at the end, just one message has given hope or comfort, or perhaps has encouraged one person to look further into their own spirituality, then my guides will rejoice and I will feel an inner glow.

Please do not read these messages in a hurry, but take your time. It won't matter if it takes you a year or more to reach the end, for if at the end you feel the upliftment these are intended to give, the hours you have spent will then have produced their reward.

I am often asked "How did you get in to Spiritualism?" My awakening came with the events described in "Ghost Story" which is at the end.

Christopher Marshall
September 2014

<u>Acknowledgements</u>

My thanks to my wife Kathleen for her continued encouragement and belief in me.

Thanks to my circle leader Joyce Balcolmb firstly for taking me on and drawing me out of myself, and then for her continued encouragement and reassurance over many years that I was truly connecting with the world of Spirit.

Here I must also thank the other members of my circle for accepting me as a friend, encouraging me all the way and reassuring me that when they say the words I write or speak are beautiful and meaningful they really mean it. Words of praise I have always found difficult and here especially so; being the only male in the circle.

<u>What's it all about?</u>

Christmas has come round again,
I ask "what is it all about?"
Santa doesn't fill my sack -
They say that I'm too old for that.
So what's it all about?

On Christmas day I'll get some presents;
Alright, so I'll give some too.
I'll stuff myself with turkey,
Then some pud. The wine I'll overdo!
So what's it all about.

It's been like this for many years;
Decorations up around November,
Then the tree early December,
Cover it with lights and stick a fairy on the top.
But what's it all about?

Booze will flow like flooded rivers,
my older brother's always sick!
Turkey never seems to finish -
I get sick of turkey and Christmas cake!
There seems no purpose to this ritual;
So what's it all about?

There's nothing really on the telly;
Mum will row with Aunty Nelly!
The noise my ears will shatter,
But when I ask them, no one knows or even
cares,

What it's all about.

A while ago it didn't matter,
I joined in with all their patter.
Now, before that day is here again
I just have to find out
What's it all about?

No one cares about my tears,
No one knows my inner fears.
It started when I lost my Timmy;
Faithful, furry friend who'd purr and love me
When I felt alone.

One day he fell ill, we took him to the Vet who said
"I'm sorry you can't take him home,
Leave him with me I'll see he doesn't suffer."
Sometimes when I cry at night it seems he's there within my arms.
But he can't be! What's it all about?

The street's lit up with decorations,
Fairies, Candles, Snowmen, Angels!
Just a minute, Angels? What's an angel?
I walk farther than before,
Suddenly I'm beside a strange building with a large door.

Within the door, all bright with lights,
The people there have made a scene.
I've never stepped within that door -
The people there are odd they say -

But now I'm drawn and cannot look away.

A stable scene, a manger filled with hay,
And in the hay a baby lies.
Looking on a man and woman -
Are they his parents?
And large animals nuzzle him and keep him
warm.
Over the manger sits an angel.
"What's it all about?" I say, and find I cry.

A gentle arm around me folds and tells me of the
little child.
His mother Mary, his father Joseph.
How he came to earth so long ago,
How He lived and died for love of me.
This was the Christ,
And Christmas day his birthday.
This is what's it's all about.
And as truth dawned within me tears fell from my
eyes.
I turned to thank the person for the story.
Then was true wonder; The angel from the street
stood there
And in his arms he held my Timmy.
Held him out to me. For seconds then I held my
Timmy as of old.
Then he took him back, and Timmy purred for
him as well.
"You see" he said, "Life goes on. Those you love
that you have lost
You will surely see again"

"But for awhile they must remain within the
Saviour's care.
There'll come a time when we'll call you back to
your heavenly home.
That time's not yet. There's much, so much for
you to do.
So make a start and come inside, learn how to
really live."

So timidly I went inside, and the angel held my
hand,
He took me to a seat and sat me down.
It was a start, I learnt to sing, I learnt to pray.
Heard stories magical.

Now I know in what went before I had the 'Mas'
Of Christmas (Mass of food and mass of
presents), but I didn't have the Christ.
Now I know I'm always loved, that there is
someone by my side.
I know it's Timmy on my bed, I need no longer
cry.

And what is best,
My life is full
And I no longer ask
'What's it all about?'

From Time Gone By

The railway before you needs crossing,
The footpath goes on over there,
You pause as you open the gate, and you listen.
In the midst of the country the silence is loud;
Yet beneath you the ground it is trembling.

As you listen the rails tremble too,
And suddenly break into song.
A joyful remembrance of time now long gone.
And a whistle breaks through the silence.

Now the song of the rails it is louder
As the train now bursts into view.
At its head a monster, a dragon,
Fire, smoke, steam it doth spew.

The roar of exhaust is exciting,
The flash of its rods so inspiring.
The fire within gleams and reflects in the sweat
of the crew.
In the darkness this manifestation
Would flash red from front and from rear;
Like Hell fire deep in the night.

Then it's gone, the exhaust fades to whisper
This machine from a long ago past
And that gets you dreaming, becoming the train:
So rare would it fail on the rail.
Determined to reach the end of the line
Some would struggle and others would falter,
Broken rods, leaky pipes? Never mind

We'll struggle along to the end of the line
And there we will rest while the crew wipes the
grime from their vests.
The passengers thank us for getting them home,
And the glow makes the hard work worthwhile.
I rest now awhile and with such loving care the
maintenance crew do their work.
Then I'm off out again on another express, it
seems that the work's never done.

Can you say the same of your life
That you'll struggle and toil through all strife
Then get your reward in a task that's well done
And the hurdles all cleared on the way?

When old and decrepit they threw me away,
And they thought that I'd never come back.
But love took my hand, and extra-ordinary men
Turned me again good as new.
My paintwork it gleams, my whistle still screams,
And again people say "Thanks for a wonderful
run".
So when you see me, brought back from the
dead,
Remember those of your own,
Don't cast them away without thought or a care
If they're old, and wheezy, and worn.
For if they are loved they will blossom and flower
And tell to you wonderful tales.
The smile that you'll get such a massive reward
For love that you give oh so freely.

Then when they are gone to God's garden on
high,
They'll look down upon you and sigh.
The love that you gave returned to you thousand
fold more,
As they steer you on life's lonely way.

Life in the River

It's snow on the mountain top, water just below.
A slow trickle whispering to those who would
listen.
Carving slowly its track to the sea.
Another stream joins it and faster it runs,
Carving a wider track now, but whispering still.
Another stream joins and still faster it runs
Carving now deeper, its voice is now louder.
And so it goes on as new streams join together,
Wider and deeper becomes then the flow
'Till no one can stop it, and none can cross over
alone.

The river flows onward, onward forever, seeking
its freedom out in the sea.
Deep now within it the creatures are stirring, the
river gives life to them all.
Now some they are gentle and bother no others,
But others are carnivores feeding at will.
You think that it's cruel this eating each other?
But think for a moment, if numbers weren't culled
the river would die,
It can't sustain all not by food or by gas, so the
smartest survive
And keep supplying the food that the others all
need.

And so in true balance the river flows on with
food and oxygen for all.

Each knows their place and accepts it; for some fish eat plants while others eat fish.
Then the big fish are food for the otter and mink
And still the balance is kept.

Now see your life as the river, you start at the top of the mountain as ice unable to move,
You melt and trickle on down ever growing, ever learning.
You are sucked now into the mainstream of life and must find your place.
Are you plant; ever growing, feeding all others by way of a chain and watching them grow?
Are you gentle fish feeding on plants but afraid for your life,
Ever looking behind you for those who would strike?
Are you fish eating fish, preying on others who do lesser tasks?
Are you otter or mink who has the last word no matter how large the prey?
Ah! Gentle friend do you see how it is and where you should sit?
For if the plant withers and dies all others die too.
So be not afraid to sit in the quiet and let others feed from you.
That life is not stressful but rewarding and true,
For you give what you are in service unending
While others may sniff and give you no thought.
When you are not there and their anchor is gone
Will they sink, swim, or be swept away.
They will rue the day that they sent you away.

A Broken World

When another person's in distress do you go
and comfort them or walk by on the other side?

If someone's lost and asks the way, a way that
you do know, do you point the path or say "I
don't know, sorry!" because the person looks
unclean or just a wee bit rough?

Hurt and bleeding will you still the flow 'till other
help arrives or stand back in case the victim
sues and let him bleed to death?

Hatred and cruelty have always been alive within
this world. Now and again love breaks through
and people smile again. But others cannot bear
the smiles and pour their scorn on love. Deny
themselves and others too of real spiritual love.
They mock at every turn 'till love turns in and
hides itself afraid to show its face.

The world grows ever darker, theft and murder
thrive, and those who caused this awful mess
wring hands in despair. It's everybody's fault but
theirs they cry, and pass ever stricter laws that
stifle speech, put fear in hearts and turn all
against each other.

The wheel at last must go full turn, the people
will rebel. Their hateful masters are undone, but
new ones will arise. Will they be bold and let love

thrive, or fearing for themselves change little and nought that matters?

The bold will let old freedoms roam, will let the people speak, then love, so long locked in their hearts will get its chance to speak. Love conquers all and will arise when least expected to take control. Love, like a shield goes on before, protecting those who give it.

Tiny sparks in a world of darkness, that is what you are, but remember too from tiny sparks a mighty fire can grow. A fire as such consumes all it can, sucking in all that is around, a mighty roaring flame. When at last that fire is spent, from there within the smoking ruin a new world must arise. A humbler world, full of respect for power it cannot see.

You know that power and understand its majesty, use your gifts wisely, spread the word and then come home to me.

A Chance Encounter

As I walk along the road
I see a sad forsaken toad.
He looks at me, is lost I see.
He's strayed too far from water.

I pick him up and carry him along the road to
water.
There I let him go and gratefully he splashes in
But moments later there upon a lily pad he sits
and croaks his thanks.
For seconds now the water clears and my heart
is lifted up for aiding one of God's creatures.
I turn now and walk upon my way and clouds my
thoughts do colour,
Black and grey the future seems, which way
shall I turn?
Then once again the toad he croaks and seems
to speak to me,
I turn and see him on his pad and a light seems
all around.

His song grows loud and the words grow clear,
"Dark clouds only enfold those who inward look,
Who see no other creature in the world that
matters more than they.
You who care, you should not fear for help will
come to you.

As surely as you picked me up and took me to the water
Someone will come and point your way,
Then if you'll take the road that's shown
Your heavy load will lift.
The choice is always yours to make,
To listen and to follow, or to turn away.
Help will come if you but ask and meet the stranger on your way.
A chance encounter, words of advice, then shines the sun.

You'll turn around and find he's gone,
This new found friend of yours.
You may fret and think him shallow – but the choice is yours,
Take his advice and bask in light, or not, and return to shadow".
Now on my way I go and it seems a shadow walks with me
But I am not afraid. Now deep within my heart the voices speak.
I know what I must do; I'll lift my head and walk with pride;
The dark clouds disperse, my fears are gone.

My trust is in the unseen shadow, my friend and teacher,
The way ahead is clearer now; it's not an easy road.
But one that I must walk to fulfil my earthly task
Then I can return and say with pride "I did my best, I tried!"

A Message

My little ones, why do you weep for things that are no more?
The past is gone for good or for bad, and in that you remember only the good, for your mind rejects the bad. For those you have known who have now passed to Spirit you should not weep but rejoice that they are now free. That they watch you from afar and whisper in your ears words you think are your own.
You, my children, are unique, it is rare we hear you ask for more, for in general you are happy with your lot. We know you sometimes look wistfully at others and their possessions, yet on the whole you do not covet, for you know that you only see the surface, and that what seems wonderful can have unhappy layers underneath.
No you do not ask for more except in the skills we offer you, the ability to speak words far wiser than your years or experience, to give comfort to those in distress, and hope to those who have none.
Yet still there are times for you when things don't go quite right and you question your sanity in pursuing this course. Rest assured that your path is true, your words and prayers are heard, that those who listen are comforted, that those you heal receive according to their need.
Trust my friends is all you need, and remember that when you look back on your life and cannot see your set of footprints in the sand, it was then

23

that we carried you. Carried you through periods of doubt and despair, carried you through illness and other trials, then set you down healed to proudly walk the path we have prepared for you. My little ones, we are here always. Trust and believe. Go forward in the light and spread the word.

God bless you.

<u>Motion</u>

Move along there, hurry up, the leader sharply
speaks
To keep the flow of people moving, ever on their
feet.
You can't stop there, you must move on for
others want to see as well.
The crocodile of people stretches far as you can
see,
Before you and behind you, it slowly trudges on.
Like a river flowing gently to the sea, it cannot
stop, it must go on.
Nothing bars this monster's way, it's roughly
pushed aside,
As the river cuts the land to straighten out its
path.
The sad thing is that as they follow few know the
destination.
They shout at those whose own free will takes
them another way.
"You'll miss the bus."
"You'll lose your way." They cry aloud, and
shuffle on another step.
Then they stare in disbelief when comes the
sharp reply,
"I'll not follow where you go. I know a better
road, a road I tread with others yet unseen.
It's my road and mine alone, though like-minded
souls may cross my road, or travel on with me
part of the way. I'll not be part of such a throng
as thee.

You're aimless, mercenary, think only of self and wealth. You think you know where that road goes?
Well think again my friend, are you at the beginning or the end?
You don't know? You can't see the beginning or the end for round and round you go.
A circle that's what you are in, doomed to wander unfulfilled into eternity.
For me a light waits at the end, and friends and loved ones too. Those who have walked their own paths and not walked with the likes of you.

Step away and follow me I'll help you find your road. But do it soon for I'll be gone along my path which will surely veer from yours."

A Lesson From Spirit

In dreams I wander far and wide in lands known
and unknown to me.
I see scenes that make me weep and from which
my eyes I'd keep.
Sorrow pain and conflict vie for precedence, and
none can win.
All around are signs and sounds of jealousy and
greed,
Of hatred and intolerance, and man's inhumanity
to man.
From these scenes I fly away, my spirit longs to
rest.
Another world I find where all is calm, all at
peace.
There I find a place to sit and rest and wonder at
the beauty of that world.
Another comes to sit by me and takes my hand.
"Do not despair." They say. "All is not lost while
those like you abide.
Kingdoms and dominions may fall and others
take their place,
Some better, others just as bad, or worse than
that which went before.
Yet there is hope; for those like you send up
their prayers and ask for better things.
Then in time those things will come to pass, but
you must trust that this is so.
For you may not live to see the change you so
desire.

Go back now, be thankful for your lot, go on as
now and spread the word
That mortal you are not. Though the flesh shall
fail and burn or rot,
That which is within goes on and never stops.
Those who love shall know light and true reward.
Those who live in darkness shall in darkness
remain
Until that time they see the light and learn to love
as well.
Then and only then may they progress though
centuries may pass.
So go back now and spread the word of light.
Know we are near and guide you, speaking
through you when we can,
Then come at last to your final rest in Spirit's
endless realm.
There you can rest awhile and be at ease until
the call comes once again.
Perhaps a guide to others you will be, or a
teacher, there in Spirit's realm.
Maybe you have much to learn before such
tasks, and study you must do.
But work and play are much the same in Spirit's
golden realm where love reigns supreme,
And joy abounds with friends and family.
Back now, and do the work you promised long
ago. Then return fulfilled, come home once
more."

Amethyst

Purple crystal, dark, mysterious, sought,
revered.
Cut and shaped, worn in rings, displayed as
found.
Thing of beauty, colour cooling, mesmerising.
Eye catching, thought provoking, mind turning.

Look into the depths and see the wonders of
nature lying there.
Let mind relax and wander far; embracing
purple, visions seeing.
Far from this madding world, slow turn the
visions in the crystal.
The world stands still; time passes by, your gaze
remains.

At peace you sit, the rushing, selfish world
forgotten,
Drawn closer still you enter in, a purple mist
engulfs you.
Then all is clear, the air is pure, the light is true,
Bright colours all around, before, behind; a
mountain.

What can you see before you?
No rushing world, no cars, no planes, no trains.
No sound or sign of war, no single person to be
seen.
No birds in the sky, no animals roam the plains.

29

Peace, pure peace, but lonesome, frightening in
its way.

Purple mist engulfs you once again.

Now you stand in a garden, wide and full of
flowers, trees, insects, birds and other animals.
Suddenly your heart lifts up; the beauty here
surpasses anything that you have known,
A gentle hand now takes your arm and guides
you onwards through the garden.
Now outside you see a bustle, people walking
everywhere.

House near and houses far, some alone, others
gathered together in towns or villages,
For it seems that you can see the whole country
as if from above.
You look in one direction and long to go there.
"Not yet", a voice within your mind doth sound,
"You've been sad, and lost.

We brought you here for rest, a moment of
peace in which we can instil hope.
Look not for the material things of life; they do
not bring lasting joy.
Look to your future home, the garden you shall
grow, the friends you'll make.
Go back now refreshed, forget your worries, trust
in the future that is to come.

Complete your service in joy, with compassion and love.
Shed no more tears, for you the world shall pass away and here you'll come to stay."

Purple mist engulfs you, the hand on your arm is withdrawn, once more you look upon the crystal with living eyes.
Know that the amethyst holds your secret, a story just for you.
When times are hard, look in again.
The swirling purple mist will remind you once more of all that you have to gain.

Be True To Yourself

The air shimmers,
A shape takes form.
Magic?
Spirit?
Who can tell?
You my friend, you ask and test.
Truth is told and your instinct knows.
Are you deceived?
No, your spirit guides are there.
Listen to them,
Know the truth,
See your path.
Many are the traps for the unwary,
For those too keen to see where nothing is.
To hear when nothing sounds.
Do not walk that path of deceit.
Trust and believe,
The words will be given.
Always and ever if you will listen.
They will hang onto your words if you speak only
truth.
Not a word will be spoken, no muscle will move.
Look around and observe when others do speak.
Is the audience restless or gripped?
Are they bored from their minds or not daring to
breathe?
Watch as they listen to you.
Know by the silence the truth that you speak.
Let the words flow freely, don't interfere.

Then will you see some cares fall away as your
truth heals the parts that do hurt.
If you can't remember the words that you've
spoken,
Don't fret for they weren't meant for you.
Be happy and glad for true service given.
For a soul given comfort no other could give.
You're an instrument only – remember that and
don't let self intervene.
Once self comes to fore the message is lost
For it's you and not spirit that speaks.
Be true to your task, seek no fortune or fame.
Whether your words bring laughter or tears,
Be sure that they bring release.
Be true to yourself, be humble and sure.
Serve well, take the pleasure from comfort oft
given.
Then at the last, when you do come home
We'll say "Well done! Come now and rest".
Your spirit we'll hold and lead it away
To the home that you've built while on earth.
There rest and recover, 'til ready once more,
A new task the Master will set.

<u>Bronze</u>

When you think of bronze what do you see?
A golden statuette or leaves on an Autumn tree?
Each a beauty of its own;
One is constant, timeless, heavy, bold.
The other light, transient, then flown to be
renewed once more when nature's cycle turns.
Bronze, a poor man's gold yet used by man for
centuries.
It is hard, yet can be moulded. A weapon tip or
ornament of beauty.
Desired or scorned as is its kindred gold.
Old or new? Now who can say? For man used
bronze in ancient times.
That ancient man was wiser than many that now
live.
He knew from whence he came and to whence
he would return.
He too had skills now long lost in time,
And would work bronze with patience and with
care.
Others came to watch him work and they would
stand and stare.
What images were in his mind? Did he know
bronze from gold or did it matter?
Colour and beauty mingled all his works, yet
most are lost, or trampled in the mud.

Think hard on that, for that which is once destroyed can never be remade.
A copy or a duplicate can never be the same, for that first was made with love,
While the rest are made with tears.

Darkened by neglect or bright with polished care.
So like the forgotten or respected soul.
The many hues that bronze can take reflect the love and care that's shown it – or not.
What colour now your soul my friend? Polished bronze or dull neglect?
So quickly does the polish fade on bronze, so likewise on the soul.

Remember whence you came and what you came to do at least once every day.
Give thanks for life and ask for guidance to do what must be done.
Do to others as you would have done to you,
Then let your soul regain that polished glow.

It will shine forth from within and draw the people close.
Some will admire, some will desire, some try to mire.
Your soul is not for sale nor there for change by others,
Show them the light and give them the tools.
Then let them choose.

They polish up their souls alone as they polish
up their shoes,
But while one is seen and worn with pride,
The other lies within and seeks not a reward,
Its golden light is hidden until it takes the sword
And strikes with utter brilliance at those who its
light would dim.
Then bronze or gold, it matters not, for it is God
within.

Bubbles

Bubbles in a chamber are just a lot of froth.
Words spoken without thought are just the same,
Time passes and decays them both,
Then who spoke the words no-one can name.
Bubbles on a river's surface go swiftly and with purpose,
Thoughtful words spread out and multiply,
An ever growing prose.
Who spoke them? Why everybody knows.
Bubbles on a windless lake just float and gather there.
Spoken words chosen with care, float on the lake of time,
Absorbed by all who hear them through the ages.
Repeated and reflected they stand the test of time.
Bubbles in the air move swiftly, sometimes near and sometimes far
'Til something breaks their surface and in a shower of droplets so they vanish.
Words float upon the breeze, drifting round corners, up or down mountains
'Til they fall on receptive ears who hear, and fears then banish.
These things are positive not negative,
For words of wisdom will endure.
Words of encouragement and love will stand the test of time.
Words of bitter anguish, of hatred or disease

Will on the wind disperse unheard,
Or be buried in the ground for ever, all forgotten.
Remember when you speak then friends,
To speak with love and joy,
For then you'll be remembered, long after this life's done.
Your memory is kept alive by good things said and done,
While those with evil in their hearts lie still, so soon forgotten.
The sun will shine upon your grave and many come to ponder
What was it within him that gave others so much wonder.
If they're quiet and listen, then they may hear your voice:
"My spirit listened and then spoke the words that you would hear.
Life goes on, you do not die – who tells you that it is a lie.
Turn from selfishness and serve the one who made you who you are.
There is comfort, there is joy within another's smile,
And your reward? The knowledge of a life lived to the full,
Of understanding nature, and all the little things that pass most men by,
Of beauty and of peace, no fear of death for love surrounds you.
Slow down and listen to your heart,
Go where your spirit wills and you will live a life fulfilled."

Crispness

Ah what pictures does that word conjure up?

Can you see fresh snow upon which frost has formed?
Purest white and untouched where you fear to tread lest you destroy the magic.

Fried bacon sizzling in the pan, crisp with wonderful aroma?

The humble potato, cut thin and fried, flavoured with salt that melts in your mouth.

The words barked forth by would be leaders, so clear to be heard, yet so void of meaning.

Sheets fresh from the wash, ironed, laid there on your bed white and crisp to the touch.

Then the words of the teachers, so clear and so sound. The words full of knowledge in you to abound. There's no room for mistakes or misunderstandings for the words all ring true, there's no mumbling or mutter. Now you must do likewise when out on the road, your words must be heard by one and by all. The words that they hear must be the words that you speak and not something guessed from a garble. So speak slowly, speak clearly, speak true. It is crispness

of diction that will make the words clear, so
make that last effort and trust, do not fear. We'll
not let you make a fool of yourself if you speak
our words calmly and true. Let them flow from
you freely like a fresh Winter snowfall. See them
carpet the floor and the frost turn them crisp,
your audience silent, afraid almost to breathe
lest they destroy the crisp carpet you've made.

Then they'll go away and remember the scene,
your words will live on in their hearts, fresh,
crisp, yet unseen. Like as the crisp doth dissolve
in your mouth your words will dissolve in their
hearts to surface at length from their own
mouths instead and pass on to another one's
heart.

Still Waters

Still are the waters of the lakes,
Waiting so patiently for you to awake.
Slumber still keeps you, dreams fill your mind,
Then you awaken, a boat you must find.

Now gently row the waters still,
The bow wave rippling to the shore,
There to break and spill.
The water's clear as crystal pure,
And depths below God's creatures fill.
Stow the oars and pause awhile.
On the water's surface let your gaze fall full.
See it glaze and mirrored become,
Another world is clear there beyond.
To the offer to join it you will succumb.

Through the mirror now you dive
And land on grass so green.

<u>Darkness Before Light</u>

Be still in the mind
Then still in the soul.
Slumbers the beast there within,
Tamed and unchained it waits there for you.
No harm can become you,
The barrier stands firm.
Long may you linger in unguided thought,
Meditate clearly and see life unfurl.
Wander the oceans and drift through the skies.
All there before you,
But where will you go?

The beast it would take you to darkness
unbroken.
Hide you away from all you hold dear.
There show so clearly the doubts and the
shudders,
The fears and the terrors for those who are evil.

But dive now into these pure clear waters,
Let your guide take your hand and show you the
way.
He'll not condemn all the things that you've
done.
He's now cleansing and teaching the right way to
go forth.

When you emerge to the surface once more
You'll understand more of the things that have
been.
Know without thinking the right things to say.
Turn others from darkness that bears no release,
Turn them to light, understanding and joy.

Then when their beast wakens they'll know no
fear
When it takes them to the darkness of night.
A warrior returns; restored to the light
Your small little band now has grown.

So listen my little ones,
Hark to the word,
Cloak yourselves deeply in light.
Then let yourself go where your beast it will take
you.
Learn in that barren dark world.
Then come and teach the things that you've
learnt,
Your light now so bright,
The darkness is gone.
The beast there within rears its head in delight;
Another of God's soldiers is ready to fight.

Do Not Despair

How can we tell you what to do or say?
Your world's in a mess from day to day.
With bombs and guns men kill and destroy,
And in the name of God is what makes it cloy.

We know that the few of you watch and despair
At the rape and the killing that's going on there.
But please my dear friends, do not blame
yourselves.
The people that matter won't listen to words.

You know that to fight in this manner is wrong,
So don't become tempted to join with the throng.
Pray for the guidance so desperately needed
To reach these sad people so that minds they
are seeded.

You cannot ignore the things that go on
But you really know what's right and what's
wrong.
So put these images out of your mind,
Concentrate hard on the things you can find.

With words of deep wisdom you can sow so
much hope
But only to those who will listen to you.
Connect with Spirit to gather those words
And with love spread them far out abroad.

You can't save them all, and this you must know.
So save whom you can, let the Spirit shine
through.
If you save only one then it's worth it to you,
And when you come home we will show you it's
true.

In the love of the Spirit you'll live all your days,
You'll feel the warm glow even on the cold days.
When it seems you're alone, that nobody cares,
Rest assured that the Spirit is still one who
cares.

The warmth and the love you'll feel all the time
As words of comfort and love flow in real time.
You'll see people change like in this rhyme
As the Spirit takes hold and says "You are mine."

So do not despair, you are never alone,
We watch and we guard you as each day is
done,
We give you the words and the gestures you
need.
Then welcome you home when you've sowed
your seed.

<u>Exhilaration</u>

Have you felt the wind a blowing in your hair so
swiftly
While you ride an open car through country-
sides of beauty?
Have you smelt the warm wet steam that from
the engine's coming
As you hang your head outside the carriage to
watch the pistons pounding?

Have you felt the Spirit's touch upon your face
so gentle?
Have you heard the Spirit's words whispered in
your ears so quietly?
Have you seen with your own eyes those Spirits
who would teach you?
Have you wondered why they come when you
are always doubting?

Yet you know that when they come your Spirit is
uprising,
It longs to know the things they know and keeps
your heart from failing.
Knowledge then is passed to you, though you
may not know it,
You only know that like the wind that takes your
hair a blowing
Your mind is lifted up so far in ways exhilarating.

Have you dived into the sea, so cold,
exhilarating?

Felt the shock of the cold sea bring close reality?
Have you stood alone upon a stage there to
receive your prize?
Heard applause for you alone while your heart it
swells with pride?

Have you bathed in Spirit's light and felt its soft
warm glow?
Have you listened to the words the Spirit speaks
so truly?
Have you kept them to yourself or passed them
on to others?
Have you seen another's tears as words of love
come through you?
Have you felt the joy the words you're given
bring to listeners?

Though exhausted, drained and spent, you go
on undaunted,
Each new message brings relief and comfort to
the list'ner.
Each smile or tear returned to you shows just
how deep their grief is.
So when at last you sink back in your chair, don't
feel sad or tired.

You've done the job we called you to, give
thanks now to your guides,
Take a long cool drink of fresh clear water, let
your breathing calm down,
Now what is it that you feel so deep within your
heart? No don't feel shame,
You've done the task, bask in real exhilaration.

Fortune

"There but for the grace of God go I."
How often have each of us looked at someone
less fortunate than ourselves and had that
thought. Our memories return to a point where
we had a choice to make. Often it was not an
easy one. To take a new job that would leave
you slightly worse off than before but where we
would be infinitely happier, or to soldier on in
misery and hope that 'something would turn up'.

For those who tighten the belt, accept the new
challenge and cast aside that which is hurtful the
immediate rewards are obvious: greater
freedom, less stress and a feeling of worth that
was previously lacking. Then what if you hadn't
taken that new post? You meet someone from
your old place who tells you things have gone
from bad to worse, everyone who can is leaving,
you did the right thing as your section was shut
down completely shortly after you left. They
themselves have just had a new job offer and
are off too. Now you realise that it was all meant,
that someone unseen had your welfare at heart
and you are better off in all ways – including
financial – than if you'd stayed.

You have time to look around and think. New
ideas occur, new opportunities arise, instead of
constantly thinking of yourself and your position
you are thinking of others and how you can help

them. Doors open that you didn't know existed, pleasure that exceeds all physical pleasure is yours as the smiles come to sad faces. You hold your head up high as you realise how much you have to offer others simply through words, or just being there.

Over your shoulder you feel the watching guiding presence, you are ready to listen to the inner voice, other doors open and you begin to understand that if you listen and follow you will never want: you may not be rich, but you will be content.

This is the richest gift that can be received, you have your eyes open and understanding is yours. Accept the gift and follow the way, others may not see or understand the gifts that are yours, they may even be a little afraid of you. No fear will be yours for you have that inner glow and understanding, your trust in the unseen is your fortune untold.

<u>Fragile:</u>

The petals of a flower disrupted by the breeze.
The flower's stem that holds them yet is broken
in a trice.
The bottle holding liquor safe is destroyed upon
a floor.
The fabric of a small aircraft, if torn, will let it
drop.
But someone beats upon my heart and they just
will not stop.

A laugh of scorn will shatter fragile faith,
Derision blur and fade a held belief.
In fiery furnace steel will melt.
In untold cold will rubber shatter.

Someone beats upon my heart and they just will
not stop.
They laugh and pour derision but they will surely
fail;
For even if my heart they stop,
My faith will never quail.

I've seen the light, I've heard the voice,
I am more strong than steel
For everywhere that I do go
My guardian goes as well.

An unusual force protects me
From all who'd do me harm,
And each time a quiver comes,

50

A panic grips your mind, will you find it again?
But the hilltop's close and you go on.
A final effort, a last gasp and you reach the top
and sit relieved,
You didn't think it would take so long, but the
view is breath-taking
(if you had any breath left that is).

Now a golden light surrounds you, your thoughts
drift and you dream.
The wilderness is a treasure trove of hidden
beauty and you can see it all.
Peace, tranquillity, knowledge. All there for you if
you will take the time and ask.
There in the light you learn the truths your busy
life has missed.

How long you sat you do not know, you stayed in
that pure light
For there was peace, and there was truth, and
all you longed to know.
No worries there disturbed you, no thoughts of
power or gain.
Just the simple things of life shown with love and
true affection
To one who'd lost the road. Shown how a slower
pace could give you so much more.

When the light fades and you awake upon that
hilltop fair,
The moon is shining brightly, your path shows up
so clearly.

Wander back now to your car and slowly return home,
Some funny looks we're sure you'll get and questions
"Where have you been?"
But you are changed for ever, and really can't explain
You went into the wilderness and climbed a distant hill.

An angel met you at the top, and while your body slept,
The angel showed you a better life, a slower life,
A life fulfilled and brimmed with joy.
Tomorrow they must come with you,
Out to the wilderness, forget the town, the shopping,
All tasks that should be done.
The angel may not come again,
But nature's show's still on, they will return refreshed,
For if you guide them well they too will see the beauty all around,
They too will strive to preserve and not destroy.

The God of possessions will be gone.
Love now must rule your hearts.

The Lonely Soul

Over the lonely hill he comes, all on his own.
The sheep and the cattle are grazing there
But no-one sees but he.
Deep in the grasses the insects do crawl
Drops of water form on the moss.
High in the air a mist hovers round,
He surely can't see where to go.
But he's trodden this path many times in his life,
And he knows in his mind where he has to go.
He could find his way there being blindfold,
He just follows the pitiful cries.
A lost sheep, or a calf, a child or a man,
It is life in distress that he hears.
Then the angel descends to that cleft in the
rocks
From where comes those sad mournful cries.
In a moment he stoops, and soft words he now
speaks,
And the weeper's sad face turns to smiles.
Lifted up by the angel they are taken away
From that lonely place on the moor,
Taken away to a place that is warm and where
food is to nourish the soul.
The rescuing angel is nowhere about for another
in need has called him.
But around the poor soul other angels abound to
give warmth and comfort at need.
When that soul is at ease then it's sent on its
way, back to the place whence it came.

For it has work still to do, some unpleasant, it's true, but the tasks it knows it must do.
When the work is completed the soul can go home,
Rest for ever with angels at hand.
Oh dear! No not for ever, there's more work to do, for now it must come and guide you.

<u>Time</u>

What is it that passes you constantly by yet you
never see?
What is there plenty of but never enough?
What can you neither start nor stop?
What makes you early or perhaps late?
What determines the change from child to adult?
What doesn't end when you die or begin when
you are born?

Enough! You should know by now the answer's
....
TIME.

Friend or foe throughout your life, it rules your
life.
Real time – the tick of the clock, measuring each
second of the day,
Telling you the time of train or bus,
Time to work or time to play,
Time to eat or time to sleep.
Can anyone ever truly forget time and trust in
truth and totality?
Even now you look at the clock, how long is he
going on?
When's the earliest I can escape?
Only another hour or two of real peace!
All these thoughts go through your minds.
In our world is no time, no deadlines, no hurry
and therefore no worry.
Try to limit the influence time has on your lives,

Don't let it rule you, if you need a moment of
quiet, then take it.
Oh we know "Easier said than done" you say,
But even a few seconds respite will help you.

Close your eyes and open your mind, feel the
love flow,
Then, when you open your eyes you will feel
refreshed,
Reassured that you are not as alone as you
usually feel.
Stronger now to face the task that must be done.
Reach for your guide, listen, give thanks for
advice,
Anywhere, any place, any TIME.

Tom Thumb

I'm small and insignificant
They think that I don't care.
They walk on me,
They stamp on me,
They nail me to the tree.

They fade away, yet I remain,
My memory still so fresh;
I threw a spanner in their works,
To dust I turned their wretched machine,
And I remain untouchable.

With written word they strike me down,
But older words prevail.
With spoken word my name deride,
But older wisdom holds the hurt at bay,
And I remain indomitable.

Who am I, and what am I
That Science can't describe?

I am he whose presence more is felt,
I am the reassuring hand upon your shoulder.
I am no ghost, as some would have you tell,
I am alive, but everywhere,
The spirit sees the need of every soul.

If you know me and I know you,
You cannot be distressed.
Just close your eyes and I am there

To comfort and advise.
I am alive and yet unseen, untouchable,
Yet still I serve you well.

Tom Thumb you feel, yet you are not!
A giant within you lies.
Cast off your doubt, and, with a shout
Proclaim aloud your size.
I am your guard, protector, mentor.

Open your ears unto my voice
And hear the words I say.
Then with confidence go forth
Know what I say is true.
Ah, true indeed, and that's the rub,
It's difficult to trust one you cannot see or touch.
But trust you must, or, like your peers
You will be truly lost,
Go through life rudderless
Steering a ragged path.

Trust in me, I'll take you straight,
And lead you on your way.
'Til at last, when life is done
You claim your just reward.
I'll lead you through the heavenly paths
Into the realm of light.

<u>Trust</u>

A simple word, but vital, if we're to live together
in harmony and peace.
For trust means relying on others as they rely on
you.
It holds together marriages and comes before
true love, for you cannot love someone you do
not totally trust.

Trust means doing the things that you say you'll
do, it also means that others do their part too.
No-one needs reminding for the job is always
done; should you forget a single task while
working at some other, a gentle nudge will send
you on so others aren't let down.

The deepest trust it comes with knowing
someone's always there to fold you in their arms
when you are down, while knowing that your
arms are there for them when they receive a
blow.

The two are one, inseparable 'till death, they
read each other's minds and know the inner
thoughts. They know when to speak and when to
listen, and, as time rolls on they closer grow, and
love, true, deep love envelops them. E'en while
living they're not apart, and though death takes
one the two remain with one guiding and
comforting the other until the allotted time when
they shall be reunited until the end of time.

Yet the greatest trust is trust in that unseen and untouchable. When you close your eyes and allow Spirit to come close, how easy it would be to dismiss it as imagination. Yet you trust and believe. Your faith sustains you even though you be mocked and knocked. In the end your life is more fruitful, more satisfying than those who reject your creed. So trust in yourselves, trust in Spirit, trust in your God, all things unseen, untouchable, and unafraid go on.

Truth

Silver the tongue that speaks slick and sly,
Tell me, O Friend, just why must they lie?
If truth is unpalatable, it must be faced;
For the lie becomes known and the speaker
disgraced.

Truth in this world is hidden, disguised,
But in spirit is open, exposed.
Where truth is hidden, trust is destroyed.
Where it is open, trust is deployed.

So much more is achieved when truth holds its
sway,
There's no reason to hide or hold an affray.
For there in the lies is the reason for war,
For as lies came in, trust went out of the door.

Remember the lesson when you are tempted;
The lie will come back to haunt and destroy,
But truth can be built upon, trust does not cloy.
Gold is the tongue that lies has pre-empted.

More value the words that are spoken with truth,
Still more those given with compassion and love.
Speak clearly, speak truly, do not be afraid,
For the truth you have spoken no person can
trade.

Understand

How often have you asked someone if they 'understand' what you have just said, received an affirmative reply, and yet looking at them, you know full well that actually they haven't understood a word you have said and are just being polite?

Now you have a dilemma! Do you tell them they are 'telling porkies'? Do you carry on as if you believe them; apparently ignorant of their lack of 'understanding'? Or do you repeat what you have just said in such a way, that the recipient doesn't realise you've given the same information again, but somehow they now really do understand what you've said?

Each of you can think of instances where you would use each of the techniques described above; however the first must come with a degree of anger while the second will almost certainly only confuse the listener further. In these two cases it is your relationship with the listener and your understanding of their character which will determine your response.

However, neither response is correct if you are trying to convey a spiritual message, only the last will do. For if you have established your connection with your guides they will know the words you need to say and you will find them without difficulty, provided you don't let your own thoughts get in the way.

Not only must your recipient understand the message you are giving, but you must understand the unique privilege you have in passing messages in this way. Do so with confidence, but humbly, with full trust in those who would speak through you. Then you will see, reflected in joy or sorrow, the truth of the words you speak. To those who receive your words with sorrow send healing thoughts, and ask for words of comfort and encouragement, but remember too, there may be a reason why your recipient is being made to show their sorrow or grief; to expose the inner self usually hidden, and thereby gain the additional support that they need and crave, though they themselves would be the last to admit it.

So understand your fellow man, understand there is a reason for the message you are giving, understand that you are only humble instruments giving service for the greater good. If you can do this then will your inner light shine wherever you are and those who need the peace you can bring will be brought to you. Have confidence in your spirit friends who will never desert you or let you down, feel joy and warmth in each contact, draw strength from it, and you shall have love even as you dispense it.

God Bless you.

Vengeance

Watch the screen and think in shame that man
has shrunk to such depravity.
A helpless child mown down, deprived of life, for
what!
A zealot's ego and his distorted view of God.
Then you "tut" and say "a shame", put on the
kettle and make another cup of tea.

"Where are our leaders?" you exclaim, then
politicians bleat and make excuses,
At best Church leaders condemn the action, at
worst they're silent.
The world waits in vain for a Spiritual lead, for
one to say, "This is all wrong!
There are no virgins for these misguided souls in
heaven.

An etheric body's all they'll be, the joys of
physical contact no longer to be experienced.
A darkness 'till they repent is all they'll see.
Far off a speck of light, but no matter how hard
they try to reach it, it stays afar.
And so will stay until the truth of love and light
breaks through."

Powerless as individuals you rage at
incompetence and inhumanity,
And weep for those that are lost. We understand
the difficulty of standing up to be counted;
For who will listen to you the humble, normal
'man in the street'?

Even if you could make your voice heard, a louder clamour would shout you down.

So softly softly must be your approach. To speak quietly and make your views known to all who'll listen.
Speak and speak again, that your words may be repeated, digested and heard.
Through the long chain your words will eventually reach those who can order a change.
They will not know the words are yours, nor will they necessarily respond the first time the words are heard, but by the third or fourth time that the words reach them they will have to take note, for your whispers will have embraced the country and will eventually embrace the world.

The voice of the Spirit is always quiet, but there is none so persistent.
Its will must eventually prevail, for the world cannot be allowed to fall again into dark ages.
So speak and be not afraid, many others are with you and the ground swell of your views cannot be destroyed. But speak only of truth; do not speak of vengeance for that would distort your message.
Remember the truth and the words "Vengeance is Mine!" saith the Lord.

His vengeance will not be the same as yours, you may not see it, but be assured that it will come.
Those who oppose his will shall fall into darkness, while those that seek light shall find it and the warmth that it brings, in abundance.

<u>Walk the Line</u>

Walk upon a line,
It stretches far away
Your purpose to define,
It leads you on your way.

That line so very thin,
So easy to fall off,
But if you are to win,
Then you must stay aloft.

Although the way may twist and turn
And all about you seems to burn,
If you stay true and on this line,
We say to you 'You'll be just fine'.

Temptation jumps up in your path,
Beckons you to leave the line;
'Downhill this way, easy path'
If you will listen to advice of mine.

Draw up straight, ignore the demon.
Take strength from Spirit, not the Heathen.
Long and hard the path you'll follow,
Let Spirit guide you to the hollow.

Here you'll find true peace of mind.
Here are others of like mind.
Here is joy, not endless sorrow
If to the path you'll cling and follow.

<u>Watch</u>

Stand still now, be alert, your watch begins.
Turn your head slowly, this way and that,
Is anything there in the distance?
Is that something there, now so close?

Can you see the ghosts all around you?
Can you hear their soft whispered words?
Do you take to your heart now their message?
Or dismiss all as tricks of the mind?

You've been learning the ropes for some time
now.
So you really should know the signs.
Are you really so blind you can't see them?
So deaf that you cannot hear the words that we
shout
Oh so clearly right in the depth of your ear?

Just now and again you will listen, and hark to
that soft inner voice.
Just now and again you will see us and your
face light up at the sight.
How is it you do not remember the calm and the
peace that you felt
When letting us in to your side, or the joy that
you felt when you glimpsed us,
And the burning of love deep inside?

These emotions are here for you always,
You just have to let us be there,

We'll not interfere with your everyday life,
But we can help you to tread the dark road.

Then come to us on the road that is light,
Recharge and be lifted by us.
You are never alone whatever you do,
Whatever the task that you face.

With love in your heart you can do anything,
Be careful to guard yourself well,
So close yourselves down, but stay open a
speck,
Then only those close can come in.

No danger you're in if you act with such care
No harm can befall you at all.
But your life will be full, you'll see beauty in all
That you see and you touch.

Those that behold you will envy your life,
For 'twill be seen that you have no strife.
But only you know that it's God in your heart
That makes you so peaceful and strong.

Water

Do you stop to consider the wonders of water?
Think for a moment where you find it and its
form:
The oceans and seas, rivers and pools, rain, ice
and snow,
Steam, hail, the little stream, spray from the
waterfall.
Some forms you love to swim in, others to bathe
and to float, for it keeps you clean.
Rivers, seas, streams and ponds contain and
support life in many forms,
And without this life you could not live.
Under pressure steam has great power and can
move mighty things.
Nothing resists the river in flood for its power
sweeps all before.
Nothing surpasses the beauty of the waterfall
with the sun's rays scattered in rainbows in its
spray.
You run from the rain, hide from the hail, can you
marvel at the shape of the snowflakes?
Each one so alike but no two the same.
Do you wonder why fish go to the bottom when
cold is about, do you know that it's warmer down
there.
All this is water, simply H 2 O with a little
deuterium mixed in for fun.

At nought degrees C, that's 32 F, you find water
as liquid, as solid, as vapour, now not many
things can do that.
Your body it is mostly water, a miracle of
hydraulics!
But even then, squash out the space – you're
half a pea and weigh the same.
Did these things all happen by chance? Why
does water freeze from the top down not bottom
up?
The Great Spirit made these, his design was
perfect, for all things function as they should.
You should respect what you have been given,
look at the perfection in each living thing. Then
ask where you fit in.
Your task is clear for human kind has lost its love
of God. It cares not what the Spirit feels; and
carelessly destroys. You where you can must
show the light of truth. These little pinpricks look
like nothing, but do not be ashamed. You hold
your faith, and tell the truth for no reward on
earth. But when to the Spirit world you come
there your reward will be.

When Love Returns

Sometimes a little smile will spread
Across a face that's long been dead
To all emotion.
The heavy heart will for a moment flutter
And words come out as just a stutter.
What memory has surfaced?
What joy has been remembered?
You cannot know, for all too soon the mask it is
replaced.

Time passes still, and the heavy heart remains.
Then, of a sudden though all the memories give
pain
A vision there appears within the mind:
The loved one lost, who was so very kind.

They speak and touch as if they were alive,
To give back joy to the life on earth they'll strive.
The vision fades, but the memories seem real,
That which was lost still lives – is this surreal?

The vision comes again, and more are words of
comfort spoken.
Can it be for real? Can now the heart that's
broken
Be restored and live again once more?
The promise of reunion is in the message core.

What proof is needed for the doubter, what will give belief?
Ah look, that which was lost is now found.
A great and lasting treasure with which they were bound.
How came it there before them when 'twas taken by a thief?

Now is the heart lifted by a sign, the will to live revived.
Now together once again, in dreams and visions every day,
Side by side they walk together, yet others see but one.
The straightened back, the cheery smile makes everybody gay.
But when asked "What's changed you?" there's nothing they can say,
For only they can see and hear and take the hand that guides.
Their friends and colleagues would not understand the Spirit,
Could not understand the joy, the hope the Spirit presence brings.
These know only spirit from a bottle, think life ends with death.
Yet back to Spirit all will go with life's last God given breath.

When the Cord Breaks

When the cord breaks and the soul departs
where will you awaken?
The silver cord binds you to your fragile body.
When the cord is severed the soul is free to
return whence it came.
But there are many places to which your soul
may journey,
Some far, some not so far.
It depends on the way you have lived your life on
earth.
No, we are not talking about the 'Fire and
Brimstone' that some of your earthly preachers
invoke, there is no Heaven and Hell as such.

The Master speaking of Lazarus and the rich
man inferred a place of torment and a place of
comfort between which no soul can pass. He
was speaking to illustrate, in a way that the
people of the time could understand, the way
that you live your life on the earth plane can
affect the soul's situation when free of the body.

There are many who think they are wonderful
servants of the Lord, and brag and boast of what
they do, yet these you will usually find covet
luxuries and comfort and will hesitate to make
sacrifices for others – even their own families.
Remember the Pharisees!

More blessed are those who serve quietly, helping others and using the gifts they have been given to give comfort, reassurance and healing. They care not what they earn, but if you observe carefully you will see that they never lack. They may be better off than some and perhaps wish for a little more, but they understand that all has to be earnt and nothing comes as of right!

These latter people, when the chord is severed, will awaken in the appropriate place for the current state of their soul, they will rest, be comforted and reassured as they adjust to the new life. Then they can go on, to learn more and serve more, to give and create both in the spheres beyond and on the earth and other material planes. Light will surround them, warm them and strengthen them; love will flood their inner being. Time will have no meaning; there will be no more conflict, no worries (except about those left behind). Truth will be there in the light, and greater understanding of all things will be theirs.

But to others; some will not accept the reality of death and will linger as shadows on the earth. They will not move forward until they accept that they must leave all that they had and go forward with nothing. Once they accept that, then a guide will come to lead them to lighter places, and that may be a long and slow journey even for those who thought they were good, for though they may pass through the lower realms of shadow their soul will not be ready for the brilliant realms of light. At each stage they must examine their lives and accept the rights and wrongs of what they did, it may even be necessary for the soul to return to a material plane before it can move forward in the spirit realms.

For those who performed real evil in their lives thinking that there would be no judgement, comes the reality that they are their own judges and must face their deeds, and the misery they caused. In shadows shall they dwell until repentance comes and they ask to seek forgiveness from those they wronged. As the wronged soul will be at a higher level, forgiveness will be forthcoming and light will fall upon the former evil one. Whether they must return, or can move slowly through the levels will depend on the former state of that soul before it departed this time for the earth plane.

The truth is that no soul is lost forever, it must eventually come to the light though that may take many physical lives or centuries of your time. In the Spirit worlds every soul must come at last to the knowledge of truth and the warmth of God's love and light.

<u>Where Shall We Go?</u>

Once there was a balanced world where order
was unchallenged.
Each knew his place within that world and kept it
faithfully.
Though some were food for others, the plants
were food for them.
Light and water for the plants and all grew
healthily.

But raw ambition, naked greed, subverted this
ideal,
The balance was undone, hunger and famine
came.
Yet none could see the cause or halt its march.
Sunlight hid by clouds of smoke, the plants they
could not breathe.

Without the plants no herbivore could feed, and
so they starved.
Their bodies for a little while fed others with big
teeth,
But then decayed as those you cannot see took
hold.
So too the end of those who prey on lesser
simpler souls.

Without the smoke life was reborn and all took
form again,
Yet no records showed what went before, and it
happened once again.

233

A third time then life was reborn and started on its way.
Yet once again the higher life showed no understanding of its prey.

You see what I am telling you, you know just what I mean,
Yet you say "What can I do? They'll not listen to such as me."
I tell you straight my friend there are many just like you
Who wish to raise a voice and say "Stop! We must maintain the balance."

So strive to pass your message, we'll see what we can do,
Mankind must learn to live within his means and to respect the other forms of life.
For be assured it's not this time he will escape the Earth.
Another cycle, two or three, before he makes his move.

You can and will escape at death into another world.
There you'll learn the greater things of life than wealth.
And when at length it comes the time for you to life return.
You may pick Earth, or some other place, it's up to you.

The task you'll chose will be for you and Earth
may not be the place.
Another world, a peaceful world for you to live
and serve.
Spreading the Master's message clear though
none will hear on Earth.
Take heart a better time and place awaits if you
will do your task.

<u>Where Am I Now?</u>

Where are you now? I hear you ask each time
you think of me.
I'm not far away, I'm right beside you, I whisper
my name in your ear.
You flick me away like an irritating fly, why, oh
why can't you hear?
I loved you so much, and more now that I'm
here, I can't bear to see you cry.

Yes I'm right there beside in a parallel world, I
can hear and see all you do.
I taught you that life goes on after death, but you
laughed and went on your way.
Now that I'm gone, you wish I was back to teach
you the things that I knew.
If you'd only believe my Spirit's alive and listen to
the whispers I make,
I could show you the truth, dry all your tears, and
make you love life once again.
Who can I send to open your eyes, to whom
would you listen instead?
No, it has to be me, and if while awake you won't
listen
Then in your dreams I'll appear as in life, and
then again as I now am.
A ghost in your mind will show you the way,
you'll waken with eyes open wide.

Will you believe? Not the first nor the second will
make your mind bend,

But the third and the forth will show that I know
of things that will happen to you.
You can't dismiss then that I'm still alive and
often walk with you all day.
Then you will know, if you call I'll be there, and
we can chat as we did once before.

Now mind to mind, but you'll hear my voice, my
child you have so much to do.
Time is awasting while you hide in your tears,
the task is still there to be done.
In a little while now you'll understand why it was
that I had to go,
Then tell your brother, your sister as well, I'm
alive and am now very well.

I go on before to prepare you a place (oh no, not
yet, to be sure),
But I've tasks to do too in this new world of mine,
and so many things I've to learn.
So pick up your feet, and dry off your tears as I
send you the pictures of heaven.
There's light all around, not a cross word
abounds, the colours and sounds are all magic.
There's a peace like I've never known (well I did
once before, before I came down to the Earth to
experience mortality once more), and it goes on
and on.
There's tears, but they're for those down below.

Lift up your heart for Mama is here, as she was
from your moment of birth.

Where Spirits Fly

Can you imagine a time with no rain,
Where the sun just shines down for all of the
day.
Then at night when you sleep, from nowhere it
seems
The moisture appears and freshens the greens.

The rivers still run and glint in the sun,
The flowers still bloom in abundance of colours
There's no shrivelled growth, no cracking of
ground
Yet the sun always shines when daylight
abounds.

After thunder and lightning and dreadful
downpours
The thought of no rain may appeal to your soul,
But then think again, after rain has come down
There's a freshness of air not there before.

When you're hot and all bothered you can stand
in the rain
And let its pure drops wash your troubles away.
Well perhaps not a downpour, for that would be
silly,
But to stand in the mist of fine rain when it's
warm
Is a pleasure you all know for sure – though it's
followed by scolding by parent or spouse.

So you see though the thunder and lightning you fear
The soft gentle rain is something to cheer.
You know that you'd miss it if it didn't come;
Though it means that the jobs in the garden aren't done.

Enjoy what you have with sensations so real,
It's the life that you have that gives it appeal.
But when you pass on, become Spirit supreme,
You won't feel the rain nor smell the sweet flowers.
Earthly sensations you'll know no more, just memories that you hold so dear.
You'll visit your family, friends and relations, and give them the signs that show you're around.
But the smell and the touch will not be the same and will seem now quite harsh to your soul,
For you've seen and you've tasted and touched now once more
The beauty the Spirit world offers to you.
The colours, the perfumes, the people you meet are now beyond wildest dreams.
They all blend together in one perfect state and the bliss that you feel is supreme.

The love that you have for those left behind is now all that draws you to earth,
To help if you can, give guidance in words whispered soft to those now asleep.
Then your earthly task done, you return to your home where beauty is kept,

Where's no fear for the future; your task now to learn, in the fullness of time
How to guide a dear soul through life from birth until death, for that's what you wish now to do.

So cherish the Earth and its quirky old ways while you can.
See all the sights and smell all the smells, let your sense of touch roam out of control.
That when your time comes you may take to the spirit the memories of all you have done,
And can say to yourself, I did my best. I lived, loved, and experienced all that I could.
Now I can rest and watch from above and help others to see as I did,
That not all is bad and not all is good and sometimes they blend in together,
But to be without rain, would be such a shame, for heavy or gentle it cleanses a lot,
And though it may not seem quite fair, the floods play their part
In showing up nature's true power, the frailty of life, that man does not rule
Is a lesson that all men must learn. The Spirit is strong and survives all these things,
And when it's released, be it joy or in sorrow, true lessons are learnt it is sure.
Use your time wisely, and live for each other, join hands in the rain and be washed.
Your Spirits will soar high up in the sky as they long to be free there once more.

Why You Must Trust

Why do you hesitate to try something new in the service of Spirit?
You should be like the duckling taken for the first time to the water.
Its mother goes down the bank and straight into the water.
It has faith that its mother will not lead it into danger and so follows.
No harm befalls it and in moments it is swimming.
This is not to say that the river or lake are without their dangers
For you know that there are predators both on the land and under water
That will take the young life if the opportunity arises.
Risks have to be taken, and the strong and alert survive.
You are like that duckling, the Spirit your mother, yet you fear to enter the water.
You paddle at the edge fearful to enter fully.
Do not waste the time my friends, for those who tarry are prey to those on land that mean harm.
Many who paddle, never make deep water. They are pulled away by the predator that is materialism.
The good life beckons and is easier than the swim in deep water and so they go not knowing what they are missing.

For those who enter the deep water there is still no easy passage,
You may have to swim against the current, dodge the predator beneath, even hide within the reeds.
Yet the water calls you into the open again and again, and you grow and mature, becoming the servants of Spirit that you dreamed of being.
Yes my friends, there are easier roads, but none that you can walk so freely and say at the end "I did so much for so many and yet many were the times I realised it not. Thank you for leading me along this path."
So enter fully into the waters my friends, trust and no harm shall come to you. Yes there are lessons to be learned, and some of those will be hard, yet the fulfilment of the tasks will fill your heart and soul with real joy and sense of achievement. You will hold your head high in all worlds, while those who feared the water, turned away, perhaps laughed and sneered at you; they will not be laughing then and will beg you to share the gifts you have. Then will you turn to them in pity to say "The gifts are not mine to give, they must be earned. You who had much now have little, ponder and learn, in time these gifts of mine may be yours as well, but they must be earned through love and trust. Greed and selfishness cannot avail you now. Yet I bless you and wish you well in your search."

Ponder this my friends when you hesitate to enter the water or hide from trials, your trust will always see you through, for we are always there to help and guide if you will listen.

<u>Your Dearest Friend</u>

As rain washes over the pavements
And takes all the dirt right away
It leaves a clean path on the walkway
To be trod in a sure footed way.

So waves of the spirit pass o'er you,
And wash all the darkness away.
So that when it is gone you can see clearly
And go steadfast on, on your way.

The sun, it may not be shining,
The Spirit you just cannot see.
But both are still there though they're hidden
By clouds sometimes thick and so black.

But the clouds will disperse given time.
The sun again warm on your back.
The spirit still hidden from all human sight,
But to you as clear as the day.

A friend there to walk on beside you,
To guide, guard and comfort at need.
No more will you fear the cold darkness
For the warmth of the spirit is there.

No more will you stumble for words to express
The feelings so deep in your soul.
No more will you find yourself speechless
When somebody tears at your heart.

Your friend he is there just to guide you
Though unseen by all others around
You will know he is there by the gentlest touch
Each time you feel emptiness near.

<u>Your Pathway is Defined</u>

Shimmering like the air on a hot Summer's day
I stand before you, but you do not see.
I speak the words, but you do not hear.
Yet I love you still.

I know that soon you'll both see and hear.
I know you'll weep at sights and sounds.
I know you care for others and will share your
knowledge.
I know you'll always speak the truth.

So trust in me and let me speak.
Give ear to me that you may hear.
Open now your mind
Let the words flow.

Freely I will speak through you,
Freely I will teach you.
Lovingly I'll watch you grow in Spirit,
Nurture you as wisdom grows.

No I do not speak just to the instrument,
But to all who hear these words.
You have been chosen one and all.
In a world of darkness you bring the light.
Though it often seems to you that your light is
extinguished,
Yet always the spark remains to be reignited at
the next opportunity.

Listen, see and feel, we keep you safe at all
times.
Trust your instincts and you'll not come to harm.
Believe in yourselves and you will grow.
Your light will grow with your confidence.

When you seem alone, forgotten, and forlorn,
Through your tears remember me.
I, your guide who loves you will never leave you,
Call on me and all troubles shall be resolved.

Ah! But you say "I've asked, and there's still too
much month at the end of the money!"
But the Spirit asks you "Have you ever really
wanted for anything?
All essentials have always been provided, even
in your darkest moments.
Proud desires for riches and possessions you do
not really need we will not satisfy.

But you have work to do, you will never hurt so
much you cannot work for us.
Trust and be faithful, seek no reward then shall
the reward be given.

Bless you."

<u>Your Pillar of Strength</u>

Pillars of strength rise before me.
Each time that I think 'It's the end'.
They rise up and stand there so powerful
I know I must go on and not bend.

Go hug these pillars that guide you.
Seek strength from what is within.
Don't question or argue the virtue,
For truth then must conquer all sin.

Unseen by others around you
Hold fast to these pillars of strength.
Though not made of material substance
They pierce through your heart like a lance.

These pillars are light just for you,
To guide you along on your way.
Yet if you could see the whole truth,
The light is a being of myth.

Yes an angel it is that strengthens you
Each time you are down in the heart.
Rejoice in the touch and the warmth
That is yours to the end of your life.

No reward is that angel demanding
For the strength that it gives each day.
But if you will smile and acknowledge his presence
The warmth you receive will be greater.

For if you acknowledge this being
And work close together with him,
Then your deeds will be great and rewarding
And peace will reside in your heart.

Ghost Story

Do you know the 'Lord's Prayer'? Can you recite it by heart without thought? Could you recite it by heart and without thought if your life was in danger? Can you say the same for your children and grandchildren?

Why do I ask? Let me recount the events of one night back in 1971 when I was young and free, had little time for the church and prayer and poo-pooed the idea of ghosts. The church teaches the idea of 'life after death.' But it is very rare for this to be portrayed as more than a hope. In the material world of today the very idea that there could be more to life than the current physical existence is usually considered laughable. Yet, yet wherever you go, and particularly when a tragedy has occurred, you find people searching, searching, searching for the proof that their loved ones still live on in another dimension. The joy and relief that they have when this proof is really given cannot be underestimated. Yet if heaven and the place where good spirits reside exists, then so too must its' counterpart where spirits of evil intention abound. Either of these may find their way to earth; while the good spirits come to guide or to visit their loved ones, those of evil intent can wreak great harm to the world and in particular to an individual, as I found out that night.

At that time I was living in a rambling semi-detached house in a rural area which I shared with two other young men. A rented property, the doorbell didn't work and the décor was generally shabby. As you entered the house there was a short hallway with a small living room to your right; the batteryless bell with disconnected wires hung above the door. Beyond the hallway you went straight into the dining room and from there crossed the stairwell to enter the kitchen. The stairs went up to the right as you entered the stairwell and at the top a landing went in two directions; one to the 3rd bedroom above the kitchen, while the other, running first above the stairs to be above the doors to the kitchen and dining room, led to a short passageway with a door immediately on the left to my bedroom while leading on to the master bedroom.

On this night I had gone to bed earlyish – about 10pm as I had no transport and my housemates were both away for the weekend. My bed lay against the passageway wall with the headboard furthest from the door. So I settled down to a hopefully peaceful slumber – no housemates, no doorbell to answer, just the peace and quiet of the country, or so I thought.

Barely had I laid down when the doorbell rang quite insistently. While I was digesting this anomaly I heard someone go and open the front door, and then voices as someone was admitted to the house. This was all very wrong and my brain couldn't work out what was happening as it was all impossible. I heard the people downstairs move into the dining room and then the stairs creaked as someone slowly began to climb towards me. It seemed an eternity as I listened to the stealthy footsteps, and my heart stopped when the footsteps stopped outside my door. Slowly the door handle turned and the door was slowly pushed open. Now my heart began to thump; a black glove appeared on the edge of the open door then its owner followed it into the room. Dressed all in black – including a black hood with just slits through which red eyes glowed, he (much too tall and well-built for a woman) slid into the room making not a sound and sidled down the side of my bed that was not against the wall. For a moment he stared into my terrified eyes and leered; I felt things change.

The man turned and walked back to where the door should have been and came back up the other side of my bed. I realised that the wall had disappeared and I was in the middle of a very large room with a low ceiling and sparse, but old and adequate furniture. A kitchen range was against the wall now running from behind my headboard for some distance in to what should have been the neighbouring house. As this 'man' came back level with my head he leered again, then raised his hands and brought them down to grip my neck. For several seconds I struggled to pull his hands away, but to no avail, then in desperation I lashed out at his body, but my fist hit nothing. It passed through his body and connected with nothing.

Realisation hit me, this man was an apparition, evil, and was trying to kill me by strangulation. I had no idea how to combat this attack but instinct (or my Guardian Angel?) told me to pray. I began the only prayer that came to my mind, "Our father," the apparition faltered and the grip on my neck eased, "who art in heaven," and he let go and backed away. "Hallowed be thy name," he backed further away and covered his eyes as a glow began to fill the room. "Thy kingdom come," he screamed, turned to vapour and vanished through a crack in the louvre window. I finished the prayer and was suddenly back in my bed within my room but covered in sweat, a soft glow lit the room. It had been a battle but my prayer had been answered, I could still feel a presence in the room, but this one held no fear. I said a prayer for protection and fell almost instantly into a dreamless sleep.

It was twenty years before I first told that story to anyone, the events are as vivid in my mind today as they were when this happened in 1971 (it is now 2014) so it was not a dream. I was fortunate, I had a little knowledge and a powerful prayer in my armoury. My fear for today is that not even this basic prayer is taught to our children and they are therefore defenceless should they be subject to such an attack.

The popularity of 'Ghost hunting' reality programs on today's television, shows that people want to believe, but for the most part do not want to admit it or ask for instruction. I'm not advocating that the 'Demons' of many popular novels exist, just that there is another dimension about which we know little but which has the potential to cause harm and distress if we do not know how to call for help that will be effective when it is most needed.

Made in the USA
Charleston, SC
29 January 2015